The Waterman/Harewood Piano Series

Piano Lessons Book Two

with **Fanny Waterman** and **Marion Harewood**

D1324126

FABER *ff* MUSIC

To the teacher

PIANO LESSONS BOOK TWO follows directly on from Book One, and continues to break new pianistic and musical ground. Each of the ten chapters introduces a particular technical or musical topic, and contains studies and exercises which provide the key to the successful performances of the pieces which follow. It is not intended that a chapter should be completed in a single lesson; the rate of progress will, of course, depend on the ability of each individual. In the later chapters there is a choice of pieces, and it is left to the teacher to select those most suitable in each case. There is also an extensive appendix of scales with their related exercises and broken chords. Their use will provide the sound technical grounding that must be acquired at this stage if the pianist is to make real progress.

We have found that marks at the end of each lesson, with a star for 80 per cent or over, and a prize at the end of term are valuable incentives. A star chart is printed at the back of the book.

The use of simple duets is recommended to encourage the pianist to sight-read and to develop ensemble playing. Suitable duets will be found in *Two at the Piano*; and a wide choice of supplementary solo pieces is also available in the *Young Pianist's Repertoire* Books One and Two, all from the Waterman/Harewood Piano Series.

To the parent

Learning to play the piano is an exciting adventure for your child, and you can help in many ways. See the instrument is well tuned. A regular time of half-an-hour upwards should be set aside for practising every day, free from distractions. The child must carefully follow the teacher's instructions, and practise daily each item to be learnt. By being present at the lessons whenever possible, you will be able to supervise home practice and keep the child's interest alive. Encourage performance of the pieces in front of people, to give your child confidence and a sense of achievement.

Ten musical commandments for young pianists

1 Practise regularly every day.
2 Watch the position of your hands and your posture at the piano.
3 Always start by practising hands separately.
4 Always start by practising slowly. Stephen Heller said: 'Practise very slowly, progress very fast.'
5 Always practise your scales with their thumb, rhythm and breaking-up exercises.
6 When you make a mistake, correct it on the spot instead of rushing back to the beginning.
7 Choose the fingering most suited to your hand, write it in your copy and keep to it.
8 Always practise with steady rhythm, using a metronome to help you to keep the pulse.
9 Listen attentively to every sound and try to produce beautiful tone-colours.
10 Follow carefully all the composers' instructions on mood, speed, phrasing and dynamics.

For American readers

The British term 'note' signifies both the written note and the tone it represents. It is used throughout this book in both senses.

© 1969, 1973 by Faber Music Ltd
First published in 1969 by Faber Music Ltd
3 Queen Square London WC1N 3AU
New edition first published in 2003
Music processed by Jackie Leigh
Cover photograph by Maurice Foxall
Printed in England by Caligraving Ltd
All rights reserved

ISBN 0-571-50211-3

To buy Faber Music publications or to find out about the full range of titles available
please contact your local music retailer or Faber Music sales enquiries:

Faber Music Limited, Burnt Mill, Elizabeth Way, Harlow, CM20 2HX England
Tel: +44 (0)1279 82 89 82 Fax: +44 (0)1279 82 89 83
sales@fabermusic.com fabermusic.com

CHAPTER ONE **Learning to run**

1 Semiquavers/sixteenth-notes

A semiquaver/sixteenth-note has two tails. It is equal to half a quaver/eighth note.

This is a semiquaver rest/sixteenth-note rest:

Fill in the note names:

Clapping duets

Clap or beat the following rhythms (the pupil and the teacher should reverse their parts):

2 Dotted notes

A dot after a note increases its length by a half:

Clapping duets

3 Scales

C major

Play the scale of C major (two octaves), hands separately, then together. Keep your fingers bent.

Short cut to learning fingering

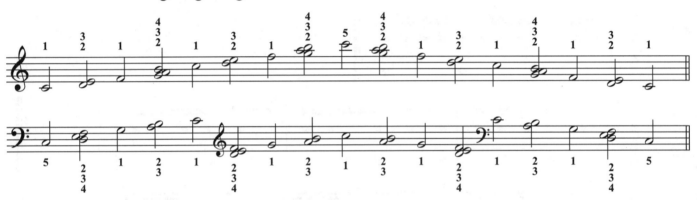

Thumb exercises

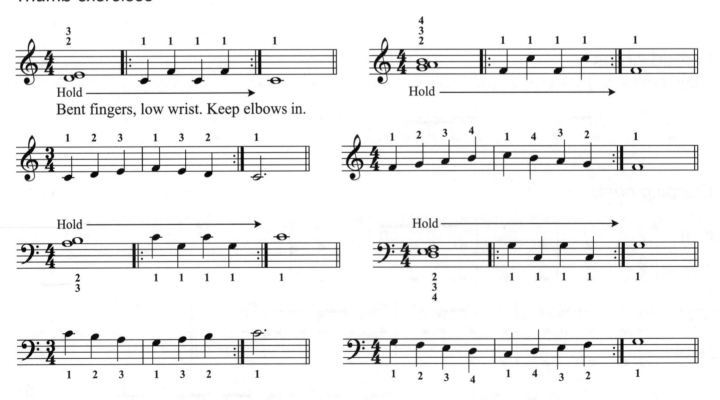

Bent fingers, low wrist. Keep elbows in.

Play also the scales of G, D and A in two octaves, with *Short cut* and *Thumb exercises*.
(See Appendix pp.56–61)

4 Running studies

Carl Czerny
(1791–1857)

a

b
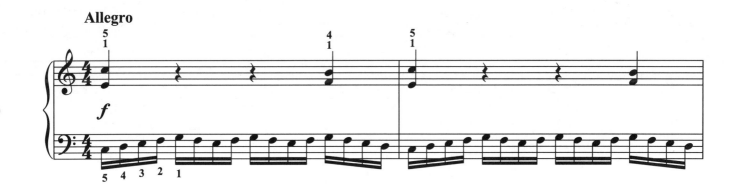

Gavotte en rondeau

Jean François d'Andrieu
(1684–1740)

CHAPTER TWO **Staccato**

1 Scales in rhythms

Practise hands separately, then together.

Practise all scales in these five rhythms. (See Appendix)

2 Staccato

Staccato is an Italian word meaning 'short and detached'.
Not all *staccato* notes are equally short. The length varies according to the mood and sound-colour (*timbre*) of the music.

(a)   (b)   (c)

In the above diagrams the black indicates the length of the sound, and the white is the silence which completes the beat.
Try playing these different lengths of *staccato* in the scale of C major, with the third finger, then use them appropriately in the study and piece which follow.

3 Study

Carl Czerny
(1791–1857)

Use *staccato* (b)

Make sure that your wrist is loose and that your hand is lifted from the wrist. Drop the hand on to each chord and immediately spring up again to the same position.

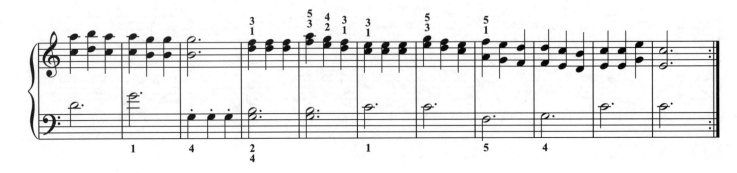

The Millwheel

Cornelius Gurlitt
(1820–1901)

Use *staccato* (a) when playing **p**

staccato (b) when playing ***mf***

and *staccato* (c) when playing ***f***

CHAPTER THREE **Breaking up**

1 Scales

E major

(See Appendix pp.62-3 for exercises)

Broken scales

The following two exercises should be practised in a regular slow rhythm, slowly at first, then faster. Snap off the last note of each group with a strong accent. All the other notes should be played lightly and softly. After playing each group think carefully what improvements you can make before playing it again. Apply these exercises first to the right, then to the left hand, and finally to both hands together.

i Note by note:

ii Beat by beat:
Beats are signposts. They help you on your journey through a musical phrase. Take care, however, not to draw attention to the signposts by giving them accents when they are not marked.

(For these exercises in other keys, see Appendix.)

2 Studies

Fifth finger study

Nekrasov

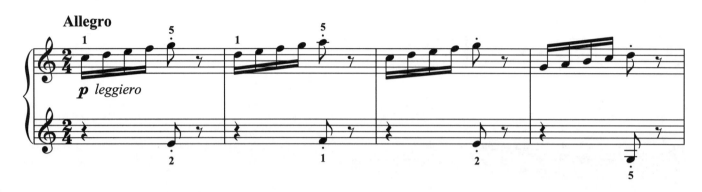

Thumb study

Ludwig Schytte
(1848-1909)

This study may be broken up and practised in the following ways.

i Note by note:

ii Beat by beat:

Scherzo

Josef Haydn
(1732–1809)

Practise this awkward corner in the following way:

Musette

Johann Sebastian Bach
(1685–1750)

CHAPTER FOUR **Equal partners**

1 Scales

Revise all the scales and exercises which you have learnt.

2 Balance of hands

Exercises

Wait at the pause and listen to the sounds dying away. (To prolong the exercise, depress the sustaining pedal before playing.)

Study

Louis Köhler
(1820–1866)

3 Counterpoint

The word 'counterpoint' comes from the Latin *punctus contra punctum*, which means 'melody against melody'. In the following pieces the right hand and the left hand have independent melodies. If you pay special attention to the dynamics, you will get the correct balance between the hands.

Fugue

Johann Pachelbel
(1653–1706)

Fugue

Ludwig van Beethoven
(1770–1827)

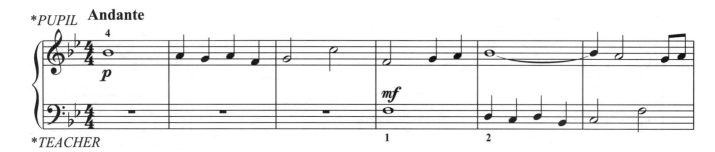

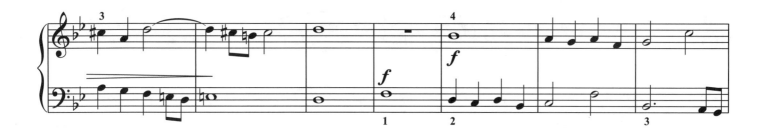

* If this is played as a duet, the teacher and pupil could reverse their parts.

Minuet *from* **The Anna Magdalena Notebook**

Johann Sebastian Bach
(1685–1750)

Here is the same Minuet with the left hand melody transferred to the right hand. The right hand melody is now in the bass.

CHAPTER FIVE **The left hand as soloist**

1 Scales

F major

Notice the irregular fingering in the right hand; the fourth finger comes on B♭ and top F.

(See Appendix pp.64–5 for exercises)

2 Chords

A chord is a build-up of sound; it consists of two or more notes played together.

Here are three very different chords:

A piano chord:

A string quartet chord:

An orchestral chord:

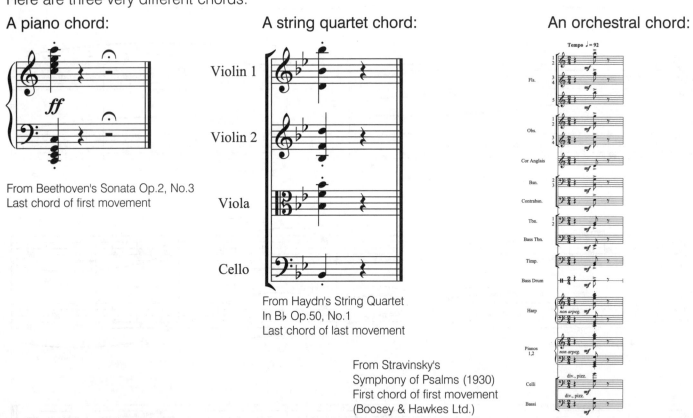

From Beethoven's Sonata Op.2, No.3
Last chord of first movement

From Haydn's String Quartet
In B♭ Op.50, No.1
Last chord of last movement

From Stravinsky's
Symphony of Psalms (1930)
First chord of first movement
(Boosey & Hawkes Ltd.)

Play the following chords. Get the feel of their shape in your hands, and listen to their different sounds.

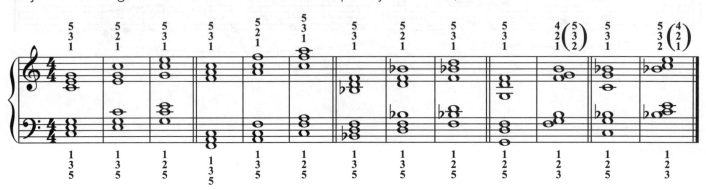

3 # Study in F

Adolf Brunner
(1901-1992)

The following chords occur in this study; learn them with their correct fingering:

The Merry Peasant *from* Album for the Young

Robert Schumann
(1810–1856)

Find the chords in this piece yourself, then copy them into a manuscript book
and practise them as you did for the *Study in F*.

Sarabande

George Frederick Handel
(1685–1759)

Practise the chords first, as you did for the other pieces.

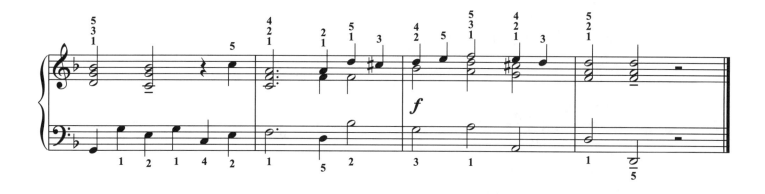

CHAPTER SIX **In the minor**

1 **The minor scale**
Pattern of the harmonic scale

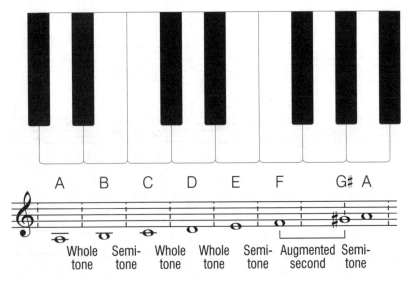

A minor

In the harmonic minor scale the third and sixth notes are a semitone lower than in the major scale.
First play the scale of A major (page 60). Then cover the black notes C♯ and F♯ with small squares of
paper, and play the scale of A minor. If you play correctly, the squares of paper will not fall off.
(See Appendix pp.66–7 for exercises)

Relative major and minor keys
Major and minor keys are said to be related to one another when they share the same key signature.
For example, compare the scales of C major and A minor:

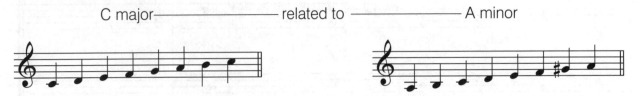

Neither has any sharps or flats in its key signature. But you will see that one note in the A minor scale
has a sharp – G♯. This is called the *leading note* (in America *leading tone*) and is sharpened to 'lead'
up to the keynote A. Every major key has a relative minor.
Note: To make the pupil aware of the different sound of major and minor, the teacher could draw
attention to the key changes in *The Millwheel* of Chapter Two.

2 # Study in A minor

Cornelius Gurlitt
(1820–1901)

Allegretto grazioso

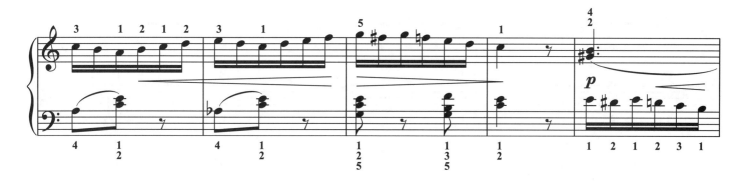

poco rit.   a tempo

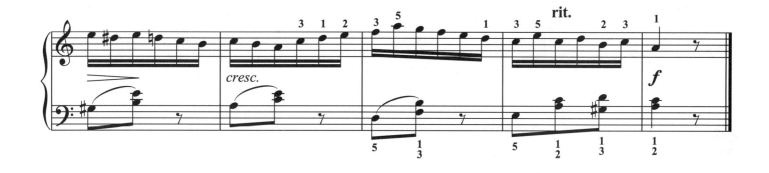

Variations on a Russian Folk Tune

Berkovitch

in E minor

Variation 1

Variation 2

Variation 3

Sarabande

Arcangelo Corelli
(1653–1713)

in E minor

Tango (Habañera)

Mátyás Seiber
(1905–1960)

in D minor

Note: The composer has left the choice of dynamics to the pianist.

CHAPTER SEVEN **Broken chords**

1 Scales

E minor   Relative major: G major

(See Appendix pp.68–9 for exercises)

2 Broken chords

A chord is said to be *broken* when its notes are played in sequence and not together.

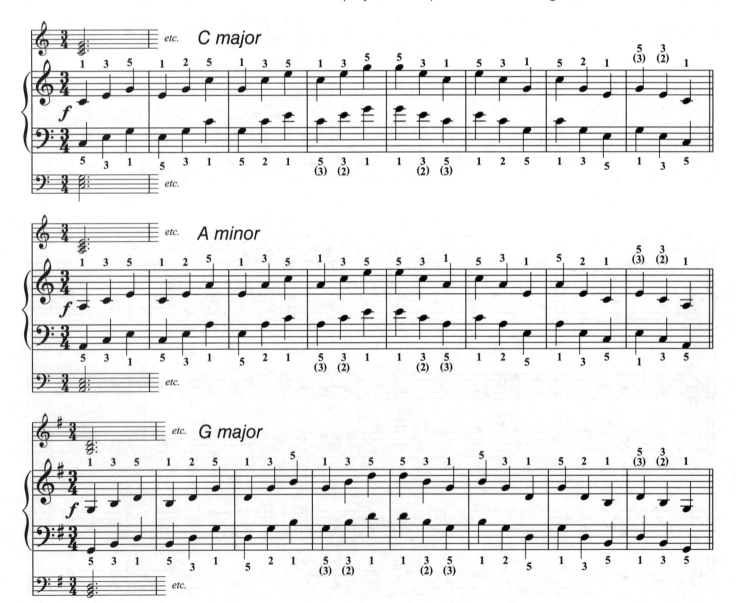

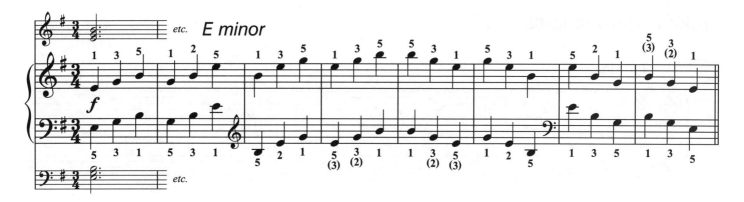

etc.   E minor

3 **6/8** time

Compare the following time signatures:

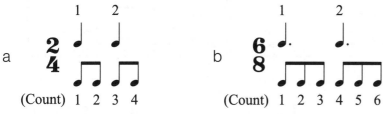

In *a* there are two main beats, each subdivided into two; in *b* there are again two main beats, each subdivided into three.

Different rhythms in **6/8**

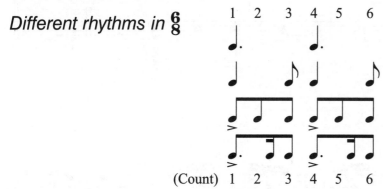

Clapping duets

4 Broken chord studies

Carl Czerny
(1791–1857)

The Return

Cornelius Gurlitt
(1820–1901)

Prelude in C

Johann Sebastian Bach
(1685–1750)

from The 48 Preludes and Fugues Book 1, No.1

Write out and play the other chords in the same way.

There are many alternative fingerings to this prelude; the teacher should help the pupil to find the one most suited to the size of the pupil's hand. The choice of speed, dynamics and phrasing is left to the performer, as it was in Bach's time.

CHAPTER EIGHT **Sounds and silences, pedals and rests**

1 Scales

D minor   Relative major: F

2 Broken chords

Four-note broken chords in C major

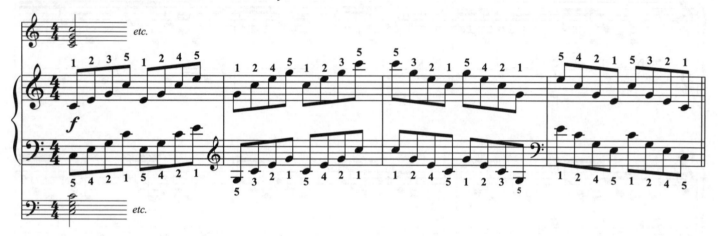

(For other keys, see Appendix.)

3 The pedal

Most pianos have two pedals.

The one on the left softens the sound; the one on the right sustains the sound and gives it a richer quality.

You are now going to learn how to use the right or sustaining pedal. Put your heel on the floor, and with the ball of the foot press the right pedal down several times, as quietly as possible. The foot should never leave the pedal.

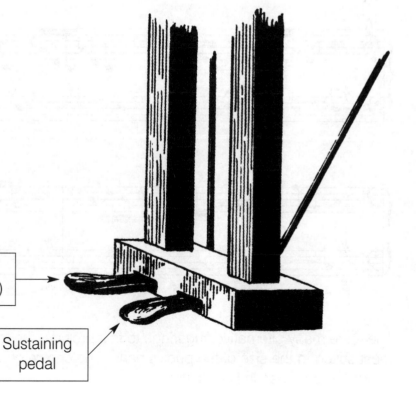

Soft pedal (una corda)

Sustaining pedal

Play the following exercises with the third finger, joining each note with the pedal as indicated:

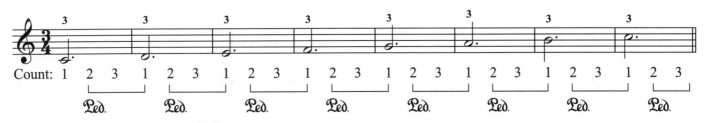

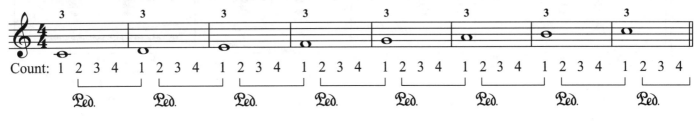

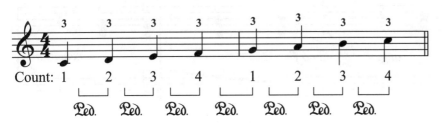

4 Silences

'Rests are part of the musical structure and sometimes as full of meaning as the notes.'
(Erwin Stein, 'Form and Performance'.)

Play these chords, feeling the silent beats:

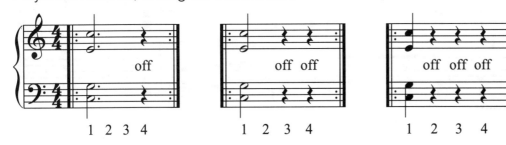

Minuet *from* Op.224, No.2

Cornelius Gurlitt
(1820–1901)

Think of your own meanings for the silences in this piece; here are some suggestions:

Soldiers' March *from* Album for the Young

Robert Schumann
(1810–1856)

In this piece the rests denote the silence between the sharp sound of the soldiers' footsteps:

Left! Right!

March

Dimitri Kabalevsky
(1904–1987)

The couplets should be played like this:

CHAPTER NINE **Con brio e cantabile**

1 Scales

Revise all the minor scales.

The chromatic scale

The chromatic scale is made up entirely of semitones; there are twelve semitones in an octave.

RIGHT HAND: Third finger on all black keys.
Thumb on all white keys *except* C and F.
Use the second finger on these notes.

LEFT HAND: Third finger on all black keys.
Thumb on all white keys except B and E.
Use the second finger on these notes.

2 Broken chords

(For other keys, see Appendix.)

3 Con brio

Carl Czerny
(1791–1857)

Three studies

4   **Cantabile**

Robert Schumann
(1810–1856)

Chorale *from* **Album for the Young**

Use the pedal to join these chords together.

Courante

Gottfried Kirchhoff
(1685–1746)

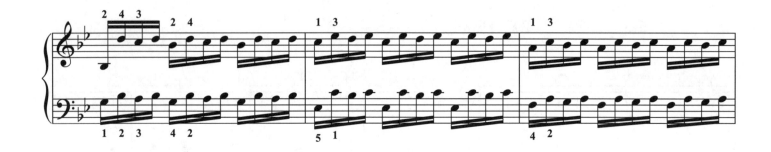

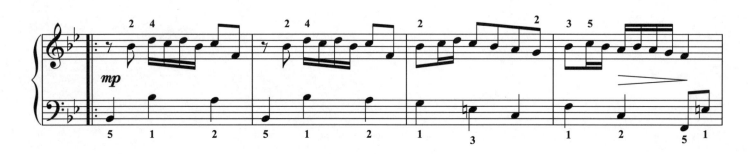

Mazurka

Alexander Gretchaninov
(1864–1956)

Reprinted by permission of Schott & Co. Ltd., London

CHAPTER TEN **Recapitulation**

1 Revision

Scales
Major scales: C, G, D, A, E and F
Minor scales: A, E and D
Chromatic scale

Broken chords

Exercises for scales
Short cut
Thumb exercises
Scales in rhythms
Breaking up   (i) Note by note
                  (ii) Beat by beat

Musical technique
Staccato
Balance between hands
Two-part playing (simple counterpoint)
6/8 time
Pedalling and sustained sounds
Rests
Couplets

2 **Couplet study**

Cornelius Gurlitt
(1820–1901)

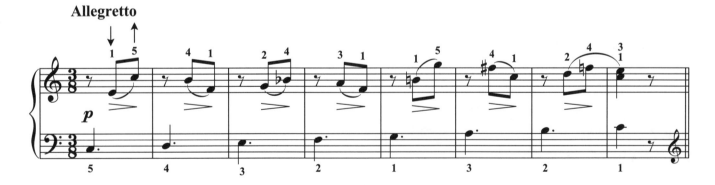

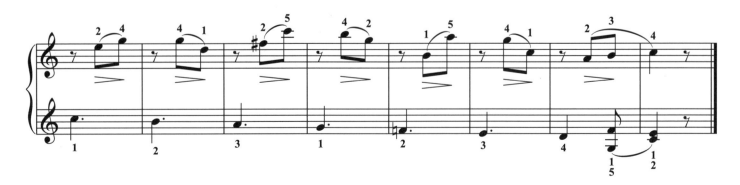

Tarantella

Charles Gounod
(1818–1893)

Italian Song

Peter Ilyich Tchaikovsky
(1840–1893)

Andantino

Wolfgang Amadeus Mozart
(1756–1791)
written at the age of eight

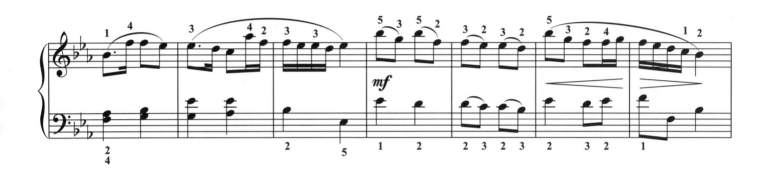

APPENDIX **Scales, exercises and broken chords**

1 C major

a *Scale*

b *Short cut to learning fingering*

c *Thumb exercises*

d *Scales in rhythms*

(v)

e *Breaking up*

(i) Note by note

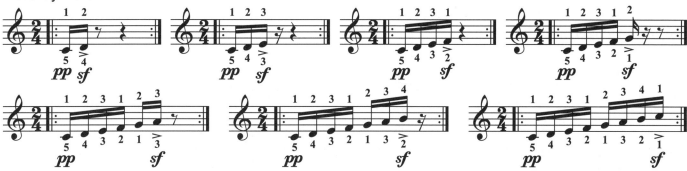

(ii) Beat by beat

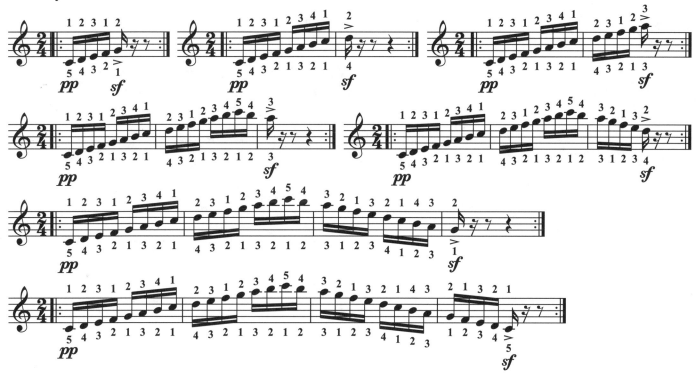

f *Broken chords*

(i)
(ii)
(iii)
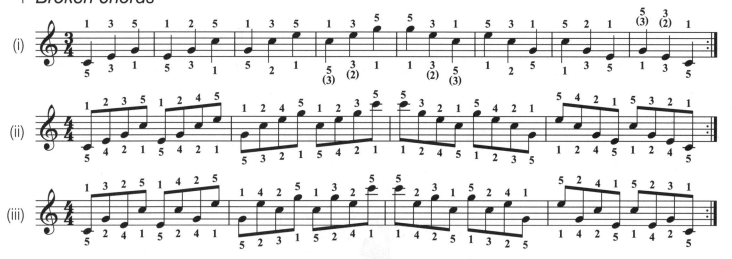

2 G major

a *Scale*

b *Short cut to learning fingering*

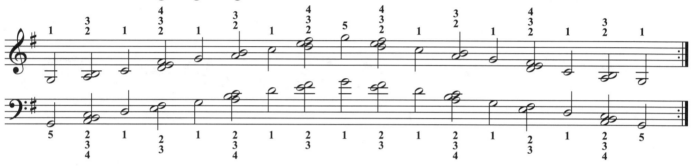

c *Thumb exercises*

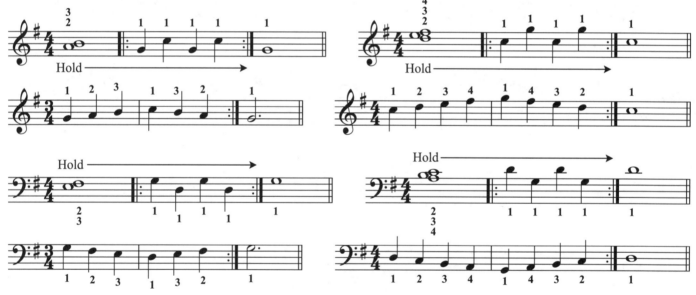

d *Scales in rhythms*

(v)

2 *Breaking up*

(i) Note by note

(ii) Beat by beat

f *Broken chords*

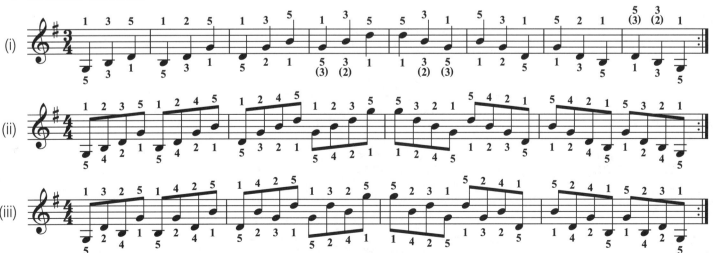

3 D major

a *Scale*

b *Short cut to learning fingering*

c *Thumb exercises*

d *Scales in rhythms*

(v)

e *Breaking up*

(i) Note by note

(ii) Beat by beat

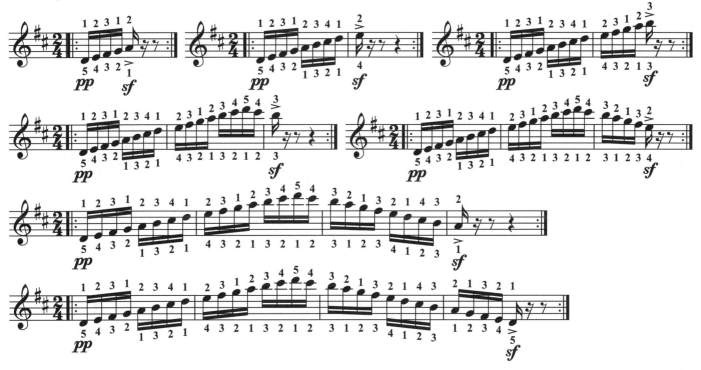

f *Broken chords*

(i)

(ii)

(iii)

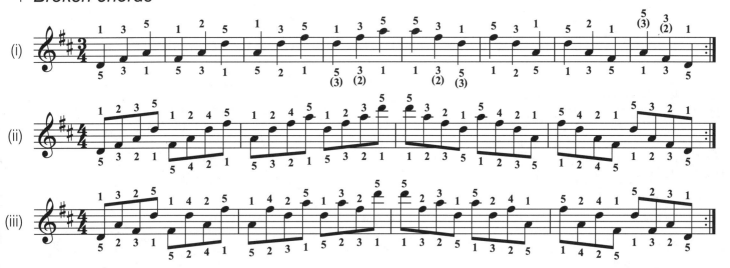

4 A major   AFC

a *Scale*

b *Short cut to learning fingering*

c *Thumb exercises*

d *Scales in rhythms*

(v)

e *Breaking up*

(i) Note by note

(ii) Beat by beat

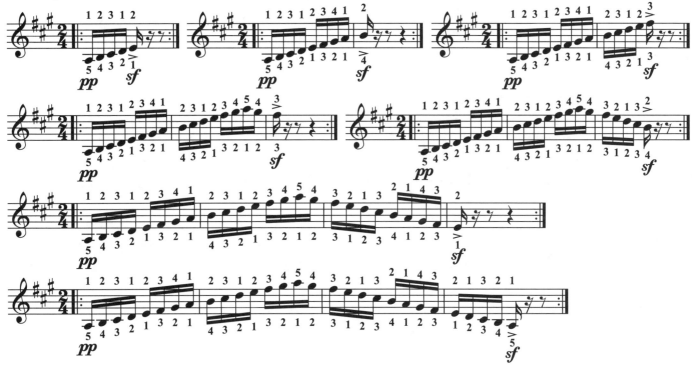

f *Broken chords*

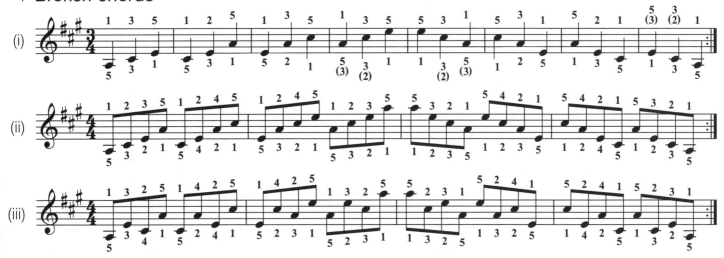

5 E major

a *Scale*

b *Short cut to learning fingering*

c *Thumb exercises*

d *Scales in rhythms*

(v)

e *Breaking up*

(i) Note by note

(ii) Beat by beat

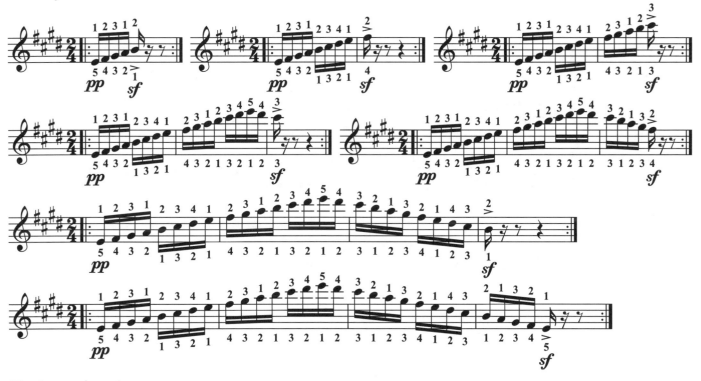

f *Broken chords*

6 F major

a *Scale*

b *Short cut to learning fingering*

c *Thumb exercises*

d *Scales in rhythms*

(v)

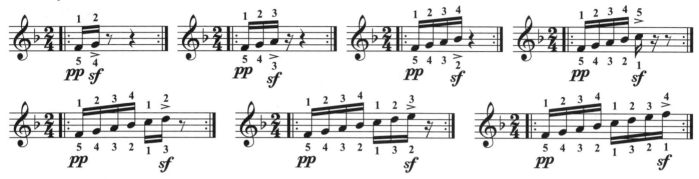

e *Breaking up*

(i) Note by note

(ii) Beat by beat

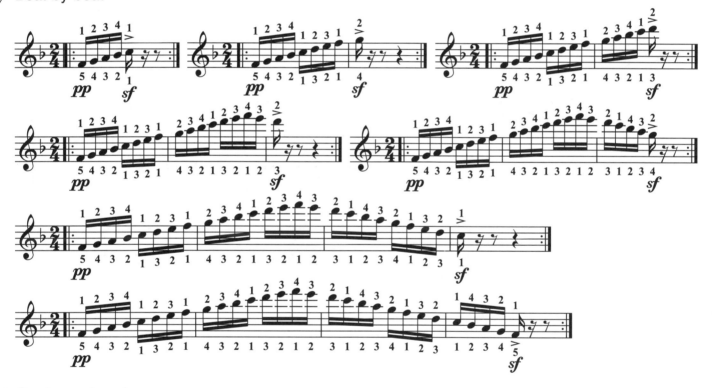

f *Broken chords*

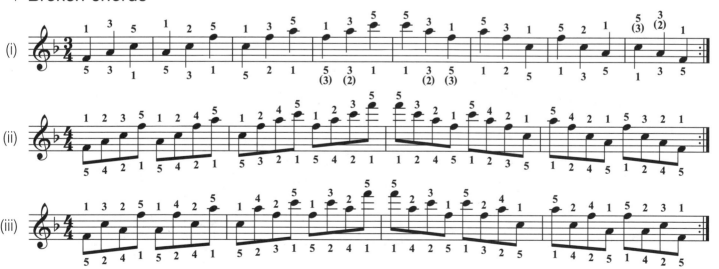

7 A minor (harmonic)

a *Scale*

b *Short cut to learning fingering*

c *Thumb exercises*

d *Scales in rhythms*

(v)

e *Breaking up*

(i) Note by note

(ii) Beat by beat

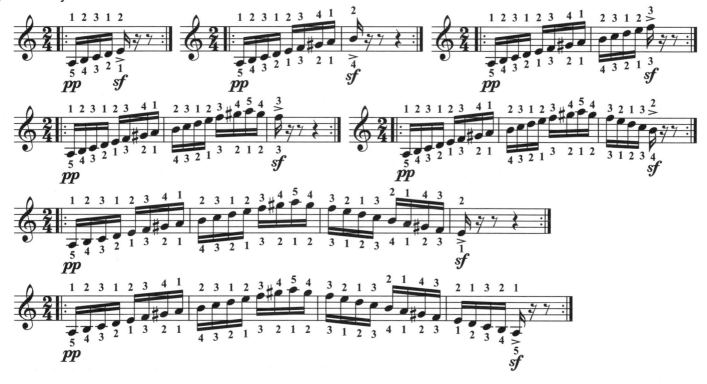

f *Broken chords*

(i)

(ii)

(iii)

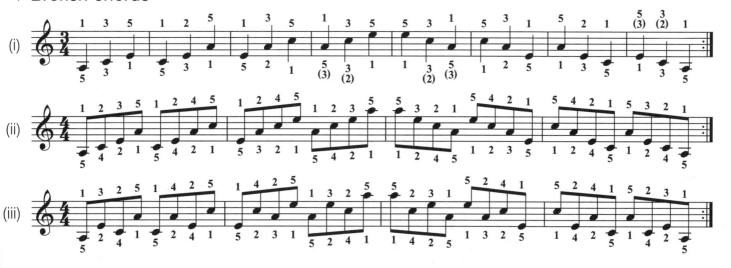

8 E minor (harmonic)

a *Scale*

b *Short cut to learning fingering*

c *Thumb exercises*

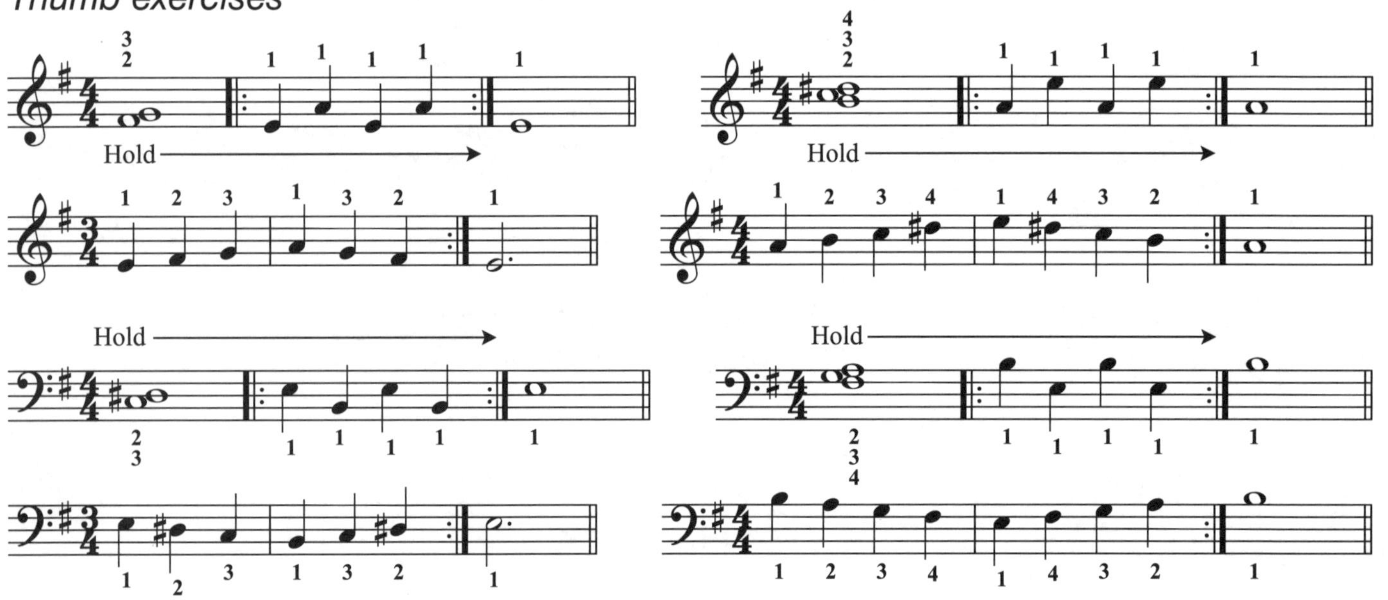

d *Scales in rhythms*

(i)

(ii)

(iii)

(iv)

v)

e *Breaking up*

(i) Note by note

(ii) Beat by beat

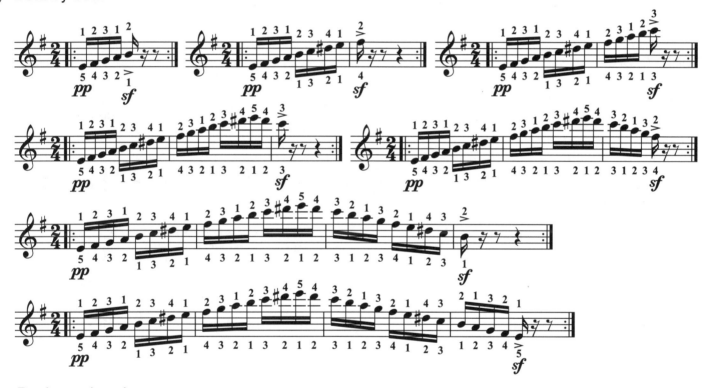

f *Broken chords*

(i)

(ii)

(iii)

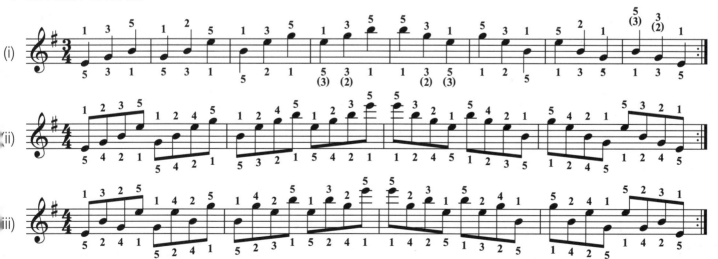

9 D minor (harmonic)

a *Scale*

b *Short cut to learning fingering*

c *Thumb exercises*

d *Scales in rhythms*

v)

e *Breaking up*

(i) Note by note

ii) Beat by beat

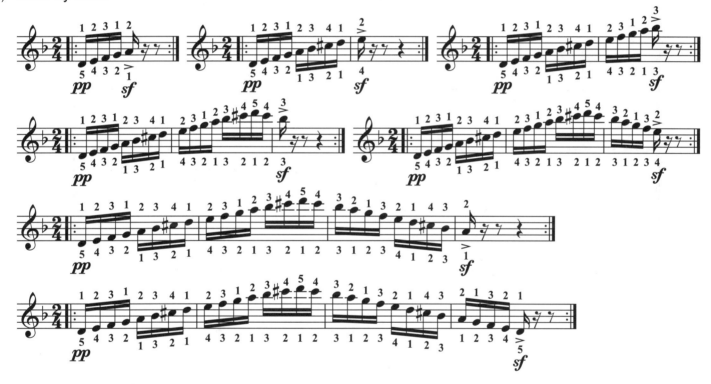

f *Broken chords*

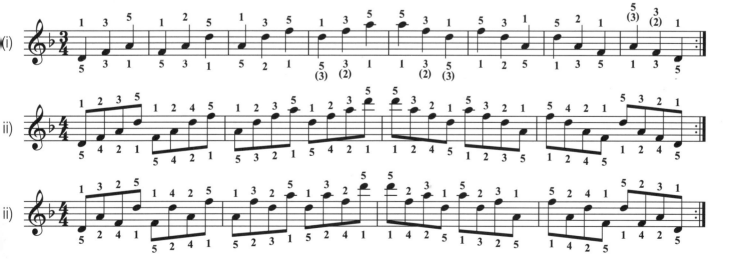

STAR CHART

Lesson	Term 1	Term 2	Term 3
1			
2			
3			
4			
5			
6			
7			
8			
9			
10			